Quilting Your Memories

INSPIRATIONS FOR DESIGNING WITH IMAGE TRANSFERS

♥

Sandy Bonsib

Martingale
& COMPANY

BOTHELL, WASHINGTON

Dedication

This book is dedicated to my family, who remind me every day that life is a series of small moments.

Acknowledgments

A very special and heartfelt thank you to the many artists from the United States and Canada who generously shared their pieces of art, their thoughts, and often their heirlooms with me. Without their generosity, this book would not have been possible.

Many thanks to my friends who have encouraged and supported me as I wrote this book, especially the "Flannel Folks and Button Babes," my small group of quilting friends, who submitted a total of twenty-two quilts for this book. Their support has been more appreciated than they know.

Thank you to Sharon and Jason Yenter, owners of In The Beginning Fabrics, Seattle, Washington, for their support and encouragement, and for giving me opportunities to teach what I love.

Thank you to Brian Basset, creator of the comic strip *Adam*, for permission to use Clayton.

And thank you to Martingale & Company for once again believing in me.

Quilting Your Memories: Inspirations for Designing with Image Transfers
©1999 by Sandy Bonsib
Martingale & Company
PO Box 118
Bothell, WA 98041-0118 USA

Printed in Hong Kong

Library of Congress Cataloging-in-Publication Data
Bonsib, Sandy
    Quilting your memories : inspirations for designing with image transfers / Sandy Bonsib.
        p. cm.
    Includes bibliographical references (p.).
    ISBN 1-56477-251-9
    1. Transfer-printing.   2. Iron-on transfers.   3. Photographs on cloth.   4. Quilts.   I. Title.
TT852.7.B866   1999
746.46—dc21   98-42874
                                               CIP

MISSION STATEMENT

WE ARE DEDICATED TO PROVIDING QUALITY PRODUCTS AND SERVICE BY WORKING TOGETHER TO INSPIRE CREATIVITY AND TO ENRICH THE LIVES WE TOUCH.

Credits
Technical Editing: Ursula Reikes
Editing and Design: Watershed Books
Photography: Brent Kane
Illustrations: Laurel Strand

Contents

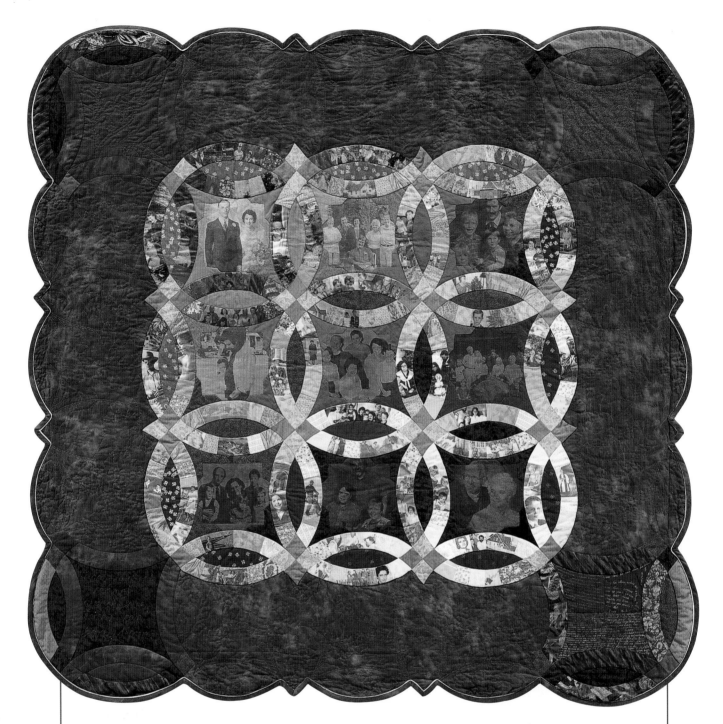

Golden Marriage *Gail Patricia Hunt, North Vancouver, British Columbia, Canada, 1994. 56" x 56"*

October 14, 1994, marked the 50th anniversary of my parents' marriage. It was—and still is—a marriage built on balances, on mutual respect, on severe hardship, and on simple pleasures. I made a quilt to honor this strong, loving bond. There is symbolism in the interlocking rings: the gold is for the "golden" anniversary and the blue increases in intensity as the relationship matures. In the borders, oak leaves symbolize strength and longevity, as well as Dad's favorite hobby, woodworking, and Mom's favorite season, fall. Acorns stand for fertility and regeneration.

Introduction

Creating a quilt that includes photographs appeals to many, many people. Yet one of the comments I have heard more than once as I have taught, demonstrated the use of image transfers, and researched information and quilts for this book is, "I haven't seen a photo transfer quilt that I've really liked." My response is, "Then you haven't seen enough of them."

Many image transfer projects in this book are not quilts in the traditional sense of the word. Many of them are wall hangings meant to be displayed. Many are intended to be heirlooms that will be cherished and passed down to future generations.

While women are often the creators of these pieces, men too seem to appreciate the finished product because they include family pictures and they're "not feminine." A father I know told me that his favorite of the many quilts his wife has made is one of their child playing baseball. Why this quilt? Because, he said, when he is 80 years old, he will look at it and remember those happy years.

Quilts often evoke strong feelings, and image transfer quilts do so even more because of the personal nature of the photographs themselves. In addition, many of us are quilters and artists—we are creative. We can combine those wonderful family photographs in interesting ways, not just reproduce a photo album. We can be selective. We can choose and combine ideas in ways that we wouldn't in a scrapbook, such as choosing only photographs of grandmother's flower garden because we lovingly remember the many happy hours we spent there with her. We can also use our wonderful fabrics, combining colors and textures that complement and enhance the photographs to provide a showcase for our memories. ♥

Our Family *Sandy Bonsib, Issaquah, Washington, 1995. 58" x 58"*

This quilt was inspired by a class, Legacy Quilts, taught by Mary Lou Weidman. The pieced blocks represent the states in which my family members were born—me in Indiana, my husband, John, in Colorado, my son Ben in Texas, and my daughter Kate in Washington. The center block represents Maryland, where John and I met. The Log Cabin border represents our log cabin home on Cougar Mountain. Machine quilted by Becky Kraus.

Sources of Inspiration

The variety of fabrics, the many subjects and occasions that can be commemorated in cloth, the many ways that images can be applied to fabric, and the numerous block and setting designs—the possibilities for quilting your memories are almost endless. Memory quilts range from traditional to contemporary, from simple to complex. In this book, I have brought together as many types of photo transfer applications as possible for your appreciation and inspiration. Hopefully, everyone will find a quilt that inspires a new project.

Quilt Styles

Image transfer quilts have many looks, not one look, so they appeal to a wide population of quilters. These quilts can be made using any kind of fabric—Amish solids, folk art plaids, springtime florals, contemporary geometric designs, youthful novelty prints, and many, many more. Thus, the person who likes Amish quilts will want to make them, and the person who likes folk art will too. Quilters who love florals can make them, as can those who are intrigued by contemporary designs. And mothers, grandmothers, aunts, and friends can make memory quilts for that special baby.

Subjects and Occasions to Commemorate

There are many occasions that can be commemorated in a quilt. The most common ones include anniversaries (especially 25th and 50th wedding anniversaries), birthdays, graduations, retirements, and weddings. Memory quilts are frequently about personal history, family history, children, childhood years and growing up, friendships, and pets. Family ideas might include family reunions, sweet-16 celebrations, or pictures of children with Santa Claus. Memory quilts can also honor a special person or chronicle a memorable family vacation.

Wear a Pink Ribbon *Elizabeth Purser Hendricks, Seattle, Washington, 1995. 41" x 49"*

This quilt is about breast cancer. Floral fabrics and soft gradations seemed well suited to this issue. Over a colorwash breast float the images of four generations of women in my family. Some have been conquered by breast cancer, others have been challenged and have survived, and several like myself have experienced the fear and surgery, and later been assured that all was benign. In the stitches of quilting the stories are told.

My students have suggested many interesting ways to create commemorative quilts:

■ At a child's birthday party, guests can write or draw with permanent markers on a tablecloth-size piece of fabric. The birthday child's photo can then be appliquéd on top.

■ A special friend's birthday can be remembered with photographs of her blowing out the candles through the years.

■ Clip art printed from a compact disk or copied from a clip art book can be added to a quilt to illustrate a theme. Animal Friends (opposite) is one such example.

■ Blocks representing the state in which each family member was born can be alternated with photographs. I did this in the quilt Our Family (page 6).

■ Grief and healing can be expressed while working on a loved one's quilt. In Wear a Pink Ribbon (page 8), Elizabeth Hendricks memorializes her family's experience with breast cancer.

■ Children's drawings for a favorite teacher can be transferred to fabric. Examples of children's art can be seen on pages 78–83.

■ Collectors can take pictures of their favorite items and use them in a quilt, as Cathy Markham did in The Teddy Bear Quilt (page 39).

Image Sources

Most books about image transfer quilts focus on photographs, but they are only one of many types of images that can be transferred to fabric. You can use

Clip art provides a rich source of images that can be used without permission.

♥

anything from art prints to found objects. Images generally fall into the following three categories:

1. NON-COPYRIGHTED IMAGES. These include most photographs, children's artwork, school papers, and other personal items such as business cards, awards, diplomas, or even airline tickets. Found objects such as leaves or dried flowers also fall into the non-copyrighted category.

2. COPYRIGHT-FREE IMAGES. These images are commonly known as "clip art," and they can be found on compact disks (for computers) and in books. Clip art designs are included in Birds of a Feather (page 13) and in Animal Friends. Clip art books may restrict you to a certain number of items per book, so when in doubt, check for this information (it's usually found in the front of the book).

3. COPYRIGHTED IMAGES. These include photographs, illustrations, and graphics that have been published in books, magazines, newspapers, comic strips, and maps; on postcards, note cards, stickers, wrapping paper, and calendars. Generally, you may copy and use these items in a quilt for your personal use only. When in doubt, request permission to reproduce it. Asking permission is not as difficult as you might think—Brian Basset, a nationally syndicated cartoonist, allowed me to use one of his characters for My Dad Thinks He's a Cowboy (page 14). Many copyright holders will allow their work to be reproduced, although some may require a one-time use fee.

Animal Friends *Sandy Bonsib, Issaquah, Washington, 1998. 51" x 51"*

Animals and plaids are two of my favorite things. These animals are an example of images transferred from a copyright-free book. I used a subtle tan plaid as a background and red plaids for the borders to give this wall quilt a warm, homey feeling. Machine quilted by Becky Kraus.

Types of Projects

Even someone who doesn't sew can make an image transfer quilt, with a little help. At a neighborhood party, when I mentioned putting photographs on quilts, two of my non-sewing neighbors said with enthusiasm, "I can make one of those!" They didn't know how to make quilts, much less how to transfer photographs to fabric, but the idea immediately sounded doable.

Beautiful artwork like this can often be found in copyright-free books.

♥

Their enthusiasm was not to be ignored. I started thinking of ways a non-sewer could make a scrapbook quilt and came up with the following advice: Buy a piece of fabric that is appealing and works well with the photographs you want to use. The fabric could be a floral print, solid, plaid;

any style will do as long as it does not overwhelm the images. Then, simply fuse the photos to the fabric and take it to a professional machine quilter to be finished. This is usually a reasonably priced option; most machine quilters will even bind your quilt for a fee. This is exactly how I made The Babies at Cougar Mountain Zoo (page 15).

Other ideas for displaying images on fabric may appeal to crafters and accomplished sewers. They include Christmas ornaments made with single photographs and fabric books for children, with pictures of grandparents, aunts, uncles, and cousins who live far away. Photographs or artwork can also be attractively displayed on pillows, either to coordinate with a quilt or as a one-of-a-kind decoration. ♥

Birds of a Feather *Lynn Ahlers, Issaquah, Washington, 1997. 36" x 29"*

I made this quilt to experiment with photo transfers, and it proves the process isn't restricted to photographs. I found these pictures in a copyright-free book and thought they were beautiful. Machine quilted by Becky Kraus.

My Dad Thinks He's a Cowboy *Sandy Bonsib, Issaquah, Washington, 1998. 50" x 62"*

Brian Basset, creator of the comic strip *Adam*, visited our local bookstore one day and drew pictures for the children there. He asked my daughter Kate what she wanted him to draw. Remembering that Father's Day was near and thinking this would be a good present for her dad, she said, "My dad thinks he's a cowboy." Brian laughed and drew Clayton, the little boy in his strip, with a cowboy hat, a devilish grin, and water pistols instead of real guns! Machine quilted by Becky Kraus.

The Babies at Cougar Mountain Zoo *Sandy Bonsib, Issaquah, Washington, 1998. 29" x 63"*

My daughter and I both love animals, especially babies. These photographs, taken by my friend and editor Ursula Reikes, are my favorites from the zoo that is down the hill from our home. Machine quilted by Becky Kraus.

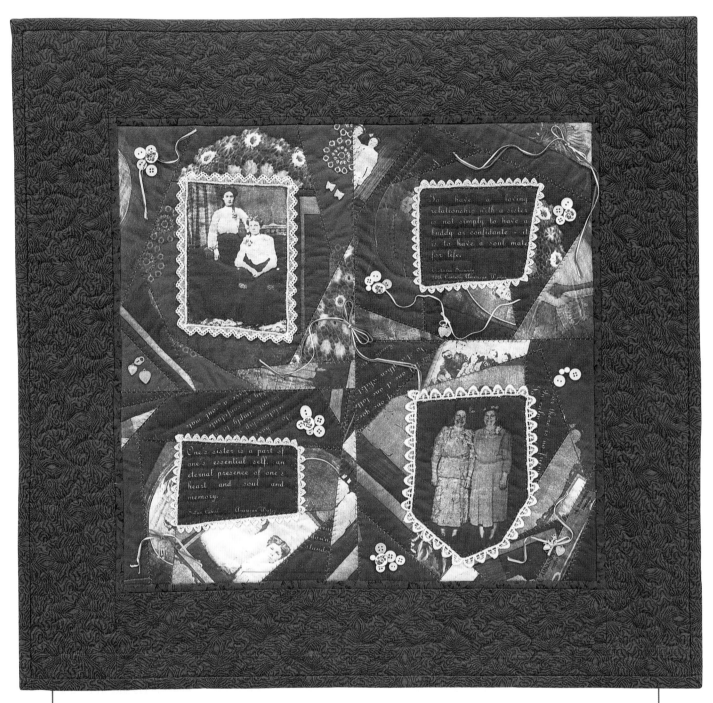

Sisters *Jean Boyd, Brockville, Ontario, Canada, 1995. 28" x 28"*

The pictures are of my grandmother and her sister, as they were as young women in Scotland and much later at a family wedding. They were constant companions throughout their lives. I transferred the photos using a cyanotype process. The text was printed on an acetate sheet, then transferred to pretreated cyanotype fabric.

Transferring Images to Fabric

TYPES OF TRANSFER PROCESSES

There are many ways to transfer images to fabric. Some processes have been available for a number of years, but older methods often involved a liquid of some sort, which destroyed the photograph or artwork being used. While this section explains only one method in detail—using image transfer paper and a color copier—some artists in this book have used other transfer methods. I'll describe these methods briefly, but if you need more specific information, refer to the books in the bibliography (page 111). Although the process may be different, the quilts and other pieces can still serve as a source of inspiration.

Image Transfer Paper

Transfer paper is not the only method of transferring images to fabric, but it is the most widely used. Anyone with access to a quilt or fabric shop or catalog can purchase transfer paper. This method involves copying your image onto the transfer paper using a color copier, then heat pressing it to fabric. For this reason, the process may be referred to as "heat transfer." The images themselves are not damaged by the process—they only get their pictures taken! Images produced on ink-jet printers are not permanent unless you use transfer paper made especially for these printers. Laser printers should produce permanent images, but they may need additional heat setting.

Cyanotype

A cyanotype is a print created by exposure to ultraviolet light. It comes from the word "cyan," which means blue; as you'd expect, cyanotypes are always blue or blue-green when completed. The method involves wetting a piece of fabric with sensitizing ingredients, letting the fabric dry, and

Friends of the Family *Jean Boyd, Brockville, Ontario, Canada, 1997. 28" x 23"*

I photocopied pictures directly onto cotton fabric, then used the transfers as the centerpieces of Log Cabin blocks. The quilt was embellished with ribbons and three-dimensional flowers.

placing a negative, a photo transparency, or a solid object such as a leaf or a stencil on the fabric and exposing it to direct sunlight or an ultraviolet lightbulb. The item on the fabric blocks the light, resulting in a white image on a blue background. The quilt Sisters (page 16) was made using this process.

Direct Printing on Fabric

You can eliminate the transfer process entirely by printing an image directly onto fabric. This process involves using a computer printer. Both color and black-and-white images can be produced, depending on the type of printer you use. The fabric needs to be stiffened before it is put through the printer. You can do this by ironing the fabric to a piece of freezer paper.

Printers and products for printing on fabric vary widely, so read all instructions carefully and always do a test piece. Friends of the Family (opposite) is an example of this technique.

Sublimation Transfer

Special heat transfer toners that contain sublimation dyes can be purchased for computer laser printers. Images are printed on paper, then heat transferred to fabric containing 50 percent or more synthetic fibers, such as polyester-cotton blends.

USING IMAGE TRANSFER PAPER

While image transfer paper is easy to use, there are some useful tricks and tips that will ensure satisfactory results. Of course, a good-quality

Color photographs can be copied in black and white by pressing the "Black" button on a color copier.

♥

original will produce a good-quality transfer, so choose images that are clear and sharply focused. If you must use a slightly blurry photograph, try reducing it; this sometimes will make it appear sharper. The sections that follow contain some of the technical information that you need to get started.

Working with Color Copiers

Transfer paper needs to be used in a color copier; do not use a black-and-white copier, because it will get too hot and melt the transfer paper. Also, certain copier models—especially older models—should not be used for transfers. Types of paper and their restrictions vary, so be sure to read all the instructions that come with the particular transfer paper you're using.

You can copy photographs in either color, black-and-white, or sepia tones. While all three can be successfully combined into one quilt, some quilters prefer to use only photographs that have the same tone. Color photographs can be copied in black and white by pressing the "Black" button (your copy machine technician should know how to do this). In addition, black-and-white photographs can be transformed to a sepia tone by selecting the Full Color button. I find that the Full Color button also produces the best color copies, rather than the automatic color setting. There are other color buttons that can shift color from normal to blue/magenta or yellow/green. Color saturation, the intensity of the color, can also be controlled by adjusting buttons from low to high.

Once you have selected your photographs, take as many sheets of transfer paper as you need, plus some extras for mistakes, to a color copier. If you are not enlarging or reducing, place as many images as you can, butted against each other, directly on the copier glass. You could also tape your images to a sheet of paper in advance. Laying out your images on paper before you copy will give you a realistic idea of how much transfer paper you'll need. It is not necessary to leave a seam allowance width when copying the image onto paper. You will do this later when you transfer it to fabric.

Other settings on the color copier that can be useful are those labeled Lighter/Darker. Generally, an image reproduced on fabric will be darker than the original. While this may not matter on some images, others may be so dark that the object of interest is difficult to see, especially if a photograph has a dark background. You can often compensate for darker images by using lighter settings. Because transfers sometimes darken when pressed onto fabric, don't be concerned if they appear on the transfer paper to be slightly lighter than you would like them. Also, don't copy a photograph in a frame; remove it from the glass or it will transfer too dark.

Make sure that the transfer paper is not bent, folded, or creased. Some curling at the corners is normal and shouldn't create paper jams, but even carefully handled paper will jam occasionally. Make sure you have an extra sheet or two of transfer paper just in case. Not all copy shops sell transfer paper; those that do may not carry the type you're using and the quality may

Use the Mirror Image setting when copying so that your image will be shown in the right perspective when it is transferred to fabric. Your transfer paper should look like this—backward—in order to read correctly on fabric.

A non-paper object, such as this handkerchief (used in the label on the back of Sue Van Gerpen's Legacy quilt, page 36) can easily be compressed directly on the glass of the copier. Remember to mirror image such objects.

♥

not be as good as the transfer paper brands sold in quilt and fabric shops.

Copy on the coated side of the transfer paper (the side without circles or lines). Press the button for "heavy paper" when using transfer paper. The copier drum seems to grip the somewhat slippery transfer paper better, resulting in fewer paper jams.

Feed each page, one at a time, into the copier, using the bypass tray. The paper should not be stacked in the regular paper trays. The 8½" x 11" paper needs to be fed into the machine on its long side (using the short side creates paper jams); the 11" x 17" paper, however, can be fed in by its short side (11").

Special Copying Considerations

A "right" perspective is important when images contain any writing, and while this is not necessarily important in every picture, I am always surprised at the less-than-obvious ones. If you make a regular copy without mirror imaging, you will produce a backward image of your photograph. To correct this, set the color copier to Mirror Image when copying onto the transfer paper. This will ensure a backward-reading image on your transfer paper and thus a right-reading image on your fabric.

Although photographs are the images most often copied, you may also consider copying three-dimensional items, such as hankies, gloves, or jewelry. I sometimes copy such items by placing them directly on the glass of the copy machine.

Enlarging and Reducing Images

If you need to alter the size of your images to fit a particular design, it is easy to reduce large photographs and enlarge small ones. Enlarging is a technique I often use because the person or object I want emphasized may be only a small part of the entire picture. You can also cover unwanted background or other elements before you copy the image to the transfer paper, or you can crop them out afterward to make the object of interest the focal point.

I have successfully enlarged 3" x 5" prints to 5" x 7" or 8" x 10" without losing clarity. The images have stayed sharp and in focus. I have even satisfactorily enlarged wallet-sized photos to 8 1/2" x 11" and larger. When in doubt about whether something will enlarge or reduce successfully, make a color copy before using the transfer paper. Keep in mind that you may lose the edge of the photo in the enlarging process if you butt it snugly against the edge of the glass, so position the image approximately 1/4" from the edge.

APPLYING PHOTO TRANSFERS TO FABRIC

Fabric Choices

Photo transfers can be applied to a variety of fabrics, but cotton is used most often. Closely woven fabrics, such as sateen or pima cotton, generally produce excellent results, especially when the transfer includes faces. The tight weave minimizes grain line so that it is not apparent, or only slightly so. Keep in mind, however, that if you are unable to find sateen or pima, almost any light-colored,

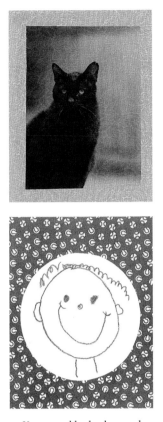

You can add a background to your image by transferring your image onto printed fabric (top) or by photocopying a picture placed over giftwrap (bottom).

♥

100-percent cotton fabric works well. Of course, you can also experiment with non-cotton fabrics. One of my students very successfully used satin.

In general, color images transfer best onto white fabrics. White enhances the colors and adds highlights, while off-white, muslin, and tan tone the images down. You may want to experiment with color—I have been pleasantly surprised at the effects that different colored fabrics have on the images I use. Black-and-white or sepia images transfer well onto off-white, muslin, and light tan, making them look even more old-fashioned. With children's drawings, silhouettes, or other dark images, I have used gold fabrics for wonderful richness. Of course, any favorite color would work, as long as it is not too dark.

Using fabrics with subtle all-over designs often means that the design will show through the photo transfer and create an interesting effect. Remember that the wrong side of the fabric can be used to produce a softer, less evident pattern. Reproducing the same photo on similar but different fabrics will produce added visual texture for the up-close viewer; Grandpa's Barn (page 23) is an example of the same image transferred on four different fabrics. Another way to create a patterned background is to purchase pieces of decorative paper or wrapping paper, place your image on it, and transfer both to fabric.

Interesting effects can also be produced with fabrics that have a coarse weave or nubby texture, such as osnaburg. The grain line is very apparent due to the weave and the dark nubs in the cloth. While it may not be what you might choose for photographs that include faces or other fine features, grain line can add visual texture to other images such as landscapes, seascapes, and skies.

Images on photo transfer paper do not transfer to dark fabrics. When I tried transferring colored images to black fabric, the color was absorbed by the black and nothing appeared except the sheen of a photograph.

While you can prewash your fabric, using cloth right off the bolt ensures that it will be very smooth, so I recommend that you not prewash your fabric before applying the transfer. Images transferred with transfer paper are permanent. They can be washed in cool or warm water, tumble dried, and ironed at a medium or hot setting. After washing, the fabric will not shrink because the photo will stabilize it. Think of it as being similar to applying a heat transfer to a T-shirt. Even though a new, unwashed T-shirt is used, the transfer is permanent and does not become distorted after washing. Many image transfers allow you to iron directly on the image without damaging it. If you are worried about whether a particular fabric or image will withstand laundering and ironing, make a test piece if possible.

The Application Process

If you have more than one image on a single sheet of transfer paper, cut them apart with scissors; be careful if you use a rotary cutter because the acrylic ruler used with it can gouge color off your transfer paper.

Parts of a transfer can be cut out. For example, in The Teddy Bear Quilt (page 39) the bear photograph originally had a dark background. Cathy Markham cut around the

A white dot or a light line that looks like a scratch can be the result of a piece of lint or thread that went unnoticed during pressing. To touch up the image, use a fine-point permanent pen that matches the color of the scratched image area.

♥

bear to eliminate the background completely, then transferred the bear to light fabric.

After trimming your transfer images, place each one face down on a piece of fabric. When cutting fabric for each transfer, leave a margin of at least 1" all around the image; for example, for a 3" x 5" photograph, the fabric should be cut at least 4" x 6". Transfers can be applied either with a home iron or with a heat press (similar to those found in T-shirt shops). The press gives superior results, because you get maximum pressure with even and consistent temperature. An iron can be used effectively if you place a book or something flat and hard under the fabric during pressing. Another option is to iron on top of a countertop covered with a towel. A soft ironing-board cover will not produce satisfactory results because you need as much firmness as possible to achieve good color saturation.

If you use a heat press, set the temperature at 375 to 400 degrees Fahrenheit; for an iron, use the hottest setting and no steam. Using steam increases the likelihood that the steam holes will leave circles on your transfer. Keep the iron moving to prevent steam holes from showing. If you have an older iron you may get better results, since the older models reached higher temperatures than newer ones do. Preheat the fabric for five to ten seconds, especially if using an iron. Preheating prepares the fabric to receive the transfer better, and eliminates wrinkles. Make sure there is no lint on the fabric or the transfer paper.

If you are using an iron, press only one image at a time. You may press more than one image if you're using a heat press, but you may find that peeling the paper off the fabric

Grandpa's Barn *Cathy Markham, Bellevue, Washington, 1998. 30" x 25"*

This barn on my grandparents' ranch holds many good memories for me. I transferred a photograph that I had taken one autumn visit onto four different fabrics to give texture to this simple quilt. The tiny Nine Patches with bits of orange reflect the branch of autumn leaves in the photo.

becomes difficult because the transfers may cool before you can peel off all of them. I limit myself to pressing no more than three images at a time when I use a heat press so that I can remove the paper while it is still hot. If the transfer paper cools and won't peel, simply reheat it for a few seconds and try again. Similarly, if there is slight distortion of the fabric (a common occurrence), you can smooth it by slightly reheating it.

When applying heat, press for 20 to 30 seconds at maximum workable pressure. With an iron, small photos that fit completely under the sole plate will transfer better than larger images. With larger ones you will need to move the iron to cover the entire image and perhaps reheat the transfer in order to peel off the paper.

Trim your seam allowance to a scant 1/4" before you sew the image transfer to another piece of fabric so underlying cloth will not show through.

♥

Trimming Your Images

Once images are transferred to fabric, trim the seam allowance to a scant 1/4", not a full measured 1/4". Trimming a little less than your actual seam allowance ensures that the fabric the photo is on will not peek through at the seam.

To create a white or light-colored frame (depending on the fabric your photo is pressed onto) around your photo, trim the fabric 1/2" from the image, then stitch with a 1/4" seam allowance when joining the piece to another one. Add dark triangles to the corners like those used on The Snowdens (opposite). Your photo will look like it came out of an old-fashioned family album! ♥

The Snowdens *Lynn Ahlers, Issaquah, Washington, 1998. 56" x 56"*

This quilt was made in memory of my grandparents Herbert and Anna Fay Snowden of Ellensburg, Washington. Their daughter Martha is my mother, and she shared some old photos of her family.

Go Kate Go

Sandy Bonsib, Issaquah, Washington, 1998. 49" x 65"

My daughter Kate played baseball for many years on boys' teams. Finally, at the urging of her girlfriends, she decided to try softball so she could play with them instead. Never one to give anything less than all her energy, Kate played with enthusiasm, game after game. Machine quilted by Becky Kraus.

Designing Your Quilt

Photo transfer quilts relate two things that aren't related—photos and fabric. To create a connection between the two, let the colors and tones in the photographs guide your selection of fabric. Repetition of color and tone will enhance whatever design you choose.

Once you have chosen all the fabrics for your quilt, step away 10 feet or more to check your choices. When you squint or look through a reducing glass, do you see the photos first? Are they the lightest part of your quilt? In the quilt Go Kate Go (opposite), you can see how Kate's white pants and her skin tones stand out against the blue and green fabrics. From a distance, do the fabrics overwhelm the photos? The fabric that looked perfect up close often reads differently when you step back. The time to find out the colors and photos don't work together is before you start piecing the two together, not after.

MAKING THE MOST OF YOUR IMAGES

When making an image transfer quilt, you want to make the photographs the center of attention. After all, they're usually the reason you've made the quilt. But it's easy for fabric with rich colors to overwhelm your images, especially those low in value or contrast. It is possible to make your images not only show but stand out, even when combined with richly colored fabrics. The following ideas are only a few of the many approaches you might try.

■ Repeat the same images, perhaps in different sizes, in your quilt. The Teddy Bear Quilt (page 39) is a good example of this approach.

■ Use many photos in your quilt. I say this with caution because a mistake I often see is trying to include so many

Watercolor Postcards *Susan Wells Hall, Mount Vernon, Washington, 1996. 35" x 35"*

This quilt was inspired by a class given by Pat Magaret, Donna Slusser, and Lorraine Torrence. While in France, I spent my time barging the Seine and Yonne Rivers, and studying *Watercolor Quilts* by Pat and Donna. I love photography and couldn't resist including my favorites from the trip in the border. They reminded me of French postcards, thus the title. Center quilted by Patsy Hanseth, borders by Susan Hall.

photographs that coordinating them with fabric and arranging them become overwhelming. Memories (page 108) shows how a scrapbook or album style of quilt can accommodate many photographs. Also, remember that you can always make a second quilt, use extra photos for pillows, or even display some images attractively on the back.

■ Select images around a theme. For example, although you may have taken many wonderful family vacations over the years, try choosing just a single year or a single location and making a quilt about that one. Souvenirs of Turkey (page 58) is an example of a single theme.

■ Enlarge your original images to emphasize a particular person or object (see Enlarging and Reducing Images, page 21).

■ Frame the image with fabrics that provide contrast in color or value. The contrast will allow the images to stand out, as it does for the images on When We Were Kids (page 105).

■ Appliqué on top of a background, rather than piecing your photo into the background. This gives a three-dimensional look, however subtle. Note how the photographs on Legacy (pages 36–37) pop out of the background.

■ Use simple, traditional blocks in combination with your photos. Hungarian Rhapsody (page 51) effectively incorporates photographs into traditional blocks. You can also feature a single photo as the center of a block and build your block and quilt around it; more complex pieced

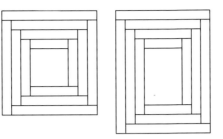

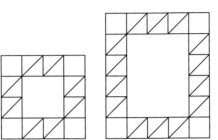

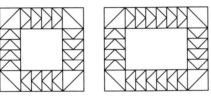

Many traditional blocks with square centers can be easily adapted to rectangular shapes.

♥

blocks work well for this purpose.

■ Create a frame by trimming 1/2" from an image so that a border of fabric frames your photo when you stitch with a 1/4" seam allowance. Jack's Quilt (page 42) illustrates this framing technique.

■ Place your photographs or artwork in the borders, as in Watercolor Postcards (opposite), rather than in the center of the quilt.

Working with Blocks

As quilters, most of us want to show off our fabric as well as our photographs, and using pieced blocks in our quilts feels comfortable and appropriate. There are many blocks that can include photographs or artwork.

PHOTOS AS THE CENTERS OF PIECED BLOCKS. When photos are the centers of pieced blocks, they can be repeated throughout the quilt. A good example of this approach is As Pieces Fall into Place (page 31).

Many pieced blocks contain centers, and while they may vary in size, most centers are squares. But the standard sizes for photographs—3" x 5", 4" x 6", 5" x 7", and 8" x 10"—are not squares, they are rectangles, so block centers that are squares need to be altered to accommodate rectangles. Some traditional quilt blocks that can be easily adapted are shown in the illustration on this page. Of course, there are many more blocks that could also be adapted to rectangular centers. For additional ideas, my favorite books to consult are *Quilts for Baby, More Quilts for Baby,* and *Around the Block with Judy Hopkins* (see Bibliography, page 111).

Julia the Pooh *Lynn Ahlers, Issaquah, Washington, 1997. 56" x 60"*

In this quilt I charted my daughter Julia from age six months to five years. I chose these photos because they were the most descriptive of her first five years. Her nickname is "Pooh."

As Pieces Fall in Place *Diane Roubal, Seattle, Washington, 1998. 62" x 56"*

Truly, this quilt was a series of fitting pieces together. The challenge was to pick shades and values of blue and yellow that showed off the photographs rather than overpowering them. The next puzzle was to fit the different-sized stars together in a pleasing arrangement, yet group them in a connected way, such as the birth announcement with the baby photo, and the photo of my husband and his brothers as children and later grown up with their wives. As I proceeded, I started to reflect on how the pieces of our past—grandparents, parents, siblings, experiences—shape who we are and what we pass on to our children. My husband and I came across all the photographs as we helped his parents move from their home of 46 years to a three-room apartment—sorting through the pieces.

PHOTOS ALTERNATING WITH PIECED BLOCKS. Photos can be alternated with pieced blocks as in Julia the Pooh (page 30). For your unpieced blocks, theme or novelty fabrics that complement the subject matter of your quilt work well. For a fishing trip, how about including pieced fish blocks? For a vacation to California, how about including Road to California blocks?

Joining Images and Blocks of Different Sizes

The photographs used in quilts are often not all the same size. Some may be 3" x 5", some 4" x 6", some 5" x 7" or larger. Of course, you can enlarge or reduce any image to correct this problem, but you can also work with photos of different dimensions. Fabric can be added to the smaller images to make them larger, or trimmed from the larger blocks to make them smaller. Pieced blocks that feature images of different sizes will create blocks that are different sizes.

The procedures for joining blocks and/or images of different sizes are the same. Arrange your images or pieced blocks on a flat vertical surface, preferably a design wall. Don't be distracted by size. Do what looks good. Starting in any section, choose two images or pieced blocks that are next to each other. If they are not the same size, you need to make the smaller one as large as the bigger one. To do this, add fabric strips or pieced-block fillers to the smaller image or block until it is as large as or a little larger than the bigger one. Trim any excess to make the images or blocks the same size, and sew them together. Make sure the newly added fabrics

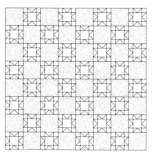

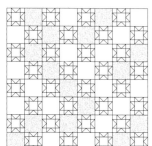

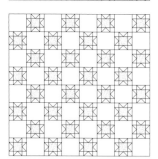

There are many ways to combine images and pieced blocks. You can alternate images and blocks, arrange images asymmetrically, or feature the image in the center of pieced blocks.

♥

blend well and that they don't overwhelm your original photos or pieced blocks.

Working with pairs of photos or blocks, put them into larger sections using the same idea—add to the smaller one and cut off the excess. Continue until your top is completed. Their Love Lives On (opposite) is an example of different sized blocks and images.

Appliqué

Appliqué is a flexible way to incorporate images into a quilt. You can appliqué or fuse images of any size onto pieced or unpieced backgrounds, and they don't need to fit next to anything so they can be placed anywhere (see illustrations on page 35).

One of my favorite appliqué methods is to create "little pillows." Photos or blocks can be stitched to a backing fabric, right sides together. Slit the back, turn inside out, and press. Attach the "pillows" to your quilt in the desired positions. This method quickly turns under seam allowances, even stubborn ones. It allows me to embellish with different types of stitches around the edges of the appliqué, since the raw edges are already turned under. Also, it gives an added dimension to the appliqué.

CONSTRUCTION CONSIDERATIONS

One of the first things that you will learn as you work with image transfers is that once an image has been fused to the fabric, the transfer area won't ease or stretch. This means it is especially important to check your measurements (and trim if necessary) so that the pieces fit

Their Love Lives On

Laurie Shifrin, Seattle, Washington, 1998. 34" x 36"

This quilt provided the perfect opportunity to honor my mother, who passed away in the early 1990s before her six grandchildren could know her. I hope that as this quilt hangs in each of my three sisters' homes, they will tell their children how much their grandmother would have loved them and what a special woman she was.

Happy 40th Anniversary *Audrey Fisher, Kirkland, Washington, 1997. 12" x 13"*

When my sister Stella had her 40th wedding anniversary in 1997, I thought, why not do a photo transfer of her wedding picture? A surprise party was held to celebrate the anniversary and this photo was on the announcement. It fit just perfectly on this printed fabric panel. Forty years ago, most pictures were black-and-white. Now my sister has a color photo quilt to enjoy.

precisely before you sew them together.

Photos on cloth do soften up after being washed, but many people do not intend to wash the quilts or other pieces that incorporate image transfers. Both hand and machine sewing and quilting can be done through the transfers, but some stiffness will remain.

Pins often leave holes in images. The holes won't come out and will also sometimes make "runs" in your image. You can try heating or ironing the transfer to make pin holes disappear, but I haven't found that method satisfactory. Therefore, I avoid pinning through the photos; instead, I pin the fabric right next to them.

Press all seams away from photos. Don't use the quilter's "press to the dark" rule. Photo transfers are often stiffer than the fabric sewn to them; if you force the seams back toward the photos, their stiffness adds bulk. Take care not to allow tucks or pleats to be pressed into your seams.

As you're sewing blocks together and folding the images, you'll notice creases, sometimes light-colored, on the photo transfers. Don't panic—they are wrinkles that can be ironed out. Many photo transfers allow you to iron directly onto the transfer; check the instructions that come with the paper.

ASSEMBLING AND FINISHING YOUR QUILT

When you are ready to put your quilt together into a top, arrange your photos and blocks on a vertical work surface, preferably a design wall, so that everything is the same distance from your eye. You will

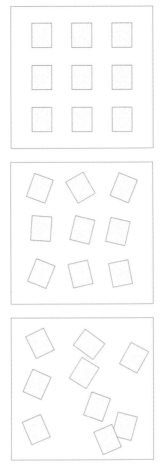

You can place appliqués in a variety of arrangements.

♥

have a better perspective this way, and you'll more easily notice things that don't look right to you. Now is the time to correct design errors. It's very discouraging to sew a top together, step away, and discover a problem after your sewing is done.

As you work on a pleasing arrangement, expect to get stumped from time to time. You'll come up with a creative solution, maybe just not right away. I suggest you walk away from your work. Leave it for a few hours or a few days. You'll think of something. Ask friends and fellow quilters for their opinions. Ask non-quilters (in my house, that's other family members) for their opinions. Non-quilters often bring a new perspective to things. They haven't learned the quilting rules as you have, so they're not afraid to break them.

Quilting

Quilting around objects or people will emphasize them. Similarly, quilting through the background will also help the people or objects to pop out and be more noticeable. You can also machine or hand quilt a "frame" around your photo.

Embellishments

Trims and accessories can provide a wide variety of ways to personalize your quilt. Such embellishments might include charms, badges, patches, buttons, coins, shells, medals, earrings, and doll accessories. You can even tuck a small music box from a craft store into a pocket. How fun to include the "Wedding March" with a 50th-anniversary quilt! Sue Van Gerpen appliquéd her

Legacy *Sue Van Gerpen, North Bend, Washington, 1998. 49" x 62"* ➤

Imagine lying on an old quilt, looking through albums of photographs, as your grandmother tells you the stories of your ancestors. Featuring photos of women in my family and vintage linens, lace, and buttons, Legacy peeks into the lives of five generations. I made this quilt for my mother, Sue DeVito, who first showed me how to make and keep memories, and for my late grandmother, Jeanette Ettswold, for telling and retelling the stories. Machine quilted by Becky Kraus.

grandmother's coin purse and handkerchief onto her quilt Legacy (pages 36–37).

Vintage fabrics, lace, silk ribbon embroidery, and appliqués are other rich enhancements. You can add life to faded areas of photographs or brighten areas you want to emphasize using fabric pens and textile paints, or you can appliqué additional photographs onto the top of your quilt.

Photo Labels

Although labels are placed on the backs of quilts, they will still be seen and appreciated. Photo labels are easy to make, since they often include just one or two images. So instead of a signature, for each quilt you create you can sign your work with your picture. If the quilt is a gift, you can add a photograph of the recipient. ♥

The Teddy Bear Quilt *Cathy Markham, Bellevue, Washington, 1998. 62" x 63"*

I love the way this photograph transferred onto osnaburg! The old teddy bear retains the fuzzy texture and fits nicely with the selection of reproduction and plaid fabrics. I was inspired to make this quilt when I stitched the little samplers and decided to incorporate them into a quilt. I especially like the warm brown tones in this quilt with a hint of old barn reds. Machine quilted by Becky Kraus.

Happier Times *Glyn Devereaux, Seattle, Washington, 1997. 39" x 31"*

This quilt was made as a gift for my sister-in-law, Linda Freeman. All the pictures are of her mother, Jean Devereaux. When Jean died, most of her pictures were divided between my husband and his sister. A few of the pictures ended up with us by default because they could not decide who should have them. I made this quilt as a way for the pictures to be shared. The themes of the quilt—gardening, crossword puzzles, and television—were Jean's favorite activities.

The Many Looks of Photo Transfer Quilts

There is no one look or style that is most appropriate for image transfers. You can make a quilt that is meaningful to you, using photographs you cherish, fabrics you love, and a style with which you feel comfortable. In this section you will see many styles. Some quilts are traditional in nature; others are contemporary. While one quilter features almost 50 years of friendship, another highlights five years of her childhood. More than one quilter features her children, while another honors her father. Children's artwork is another popular subject. Accordingly, one quilter featured a refrigerator with children's art and photographs on it, just like my real one at home! Special memories of Santa, a trip, family history; comments on people and love and life—these are all on the quilts in the pages that follow and the examples you've already seen. The quilters who made them have shared their passions in fabric. ♥

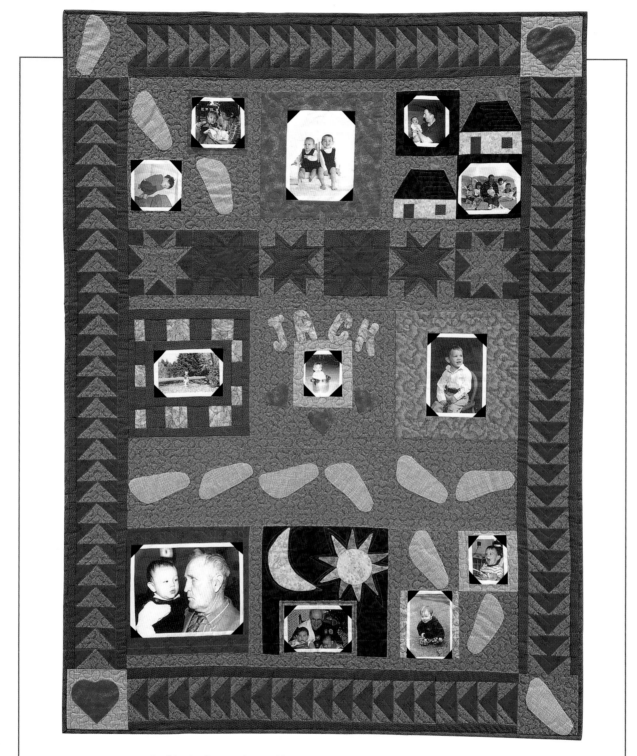

Jack's Quilt *Jennifer Cockburn, Seattle, Washington, 1998. 48" x 66"*

I made this quilt for and with my two-year-old son Jack. When I sat down to sketch and plan this quilt, Jack would color and scribble, too. He also insisted that I trace the outline of his feet. I incorporated them into this quilt, together with his photos and drawings, so this truly is Jack's quilt. Machine quilted by Becky Kraus.

Traditional Looks

Quilts that are traditional in style feature classic quilt blocks in traditional settings. Blocks range from simple squares and triangles to a variety of well-known blocks that include stars, log cabins, and more. While some quilters have chosen to repeat traditional blocks in their quilts, others have chosen a sampler style. Some quilters have added words—embroidered, appliquéd, or stamped—to enhance and personalize their pieces even more.

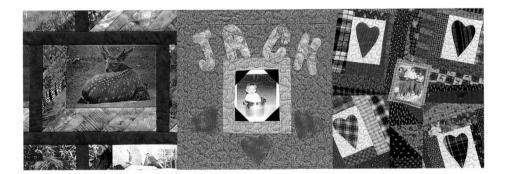

My Grandma Hattie ➤

Robin Hall, Seattle, Washington, 1998. 32" x 32"

When In The Beginning Fabrics, a store in Seattle, Washington, issued a quilt challenge using the Grandma Hattie and the Quilt Show fabric line, I couldn't resist: I had a real Grandma Hattie! She died before I was born, so I've only known her through a photograph album of my dad's. As soon as I saw the Grandma Hattie fabric, I knew what I wanted to do: the little figures holding up the quilts were perfect for framing photographs of my grandma. I cut out the quilts, then reverse-appliquéd the photo transfers in their places. They became the centers for the lopsided logs I used to complete each block. I loved doing this project because by the time it was completed, I felt a lot closer to a part of my family I never had a chance to know.

◄ ***Girlfriends*** *Sue Van Gerpen, North Bend, Washington, 1998. 51" x 54"*

Girlfriends features eight childhood friends who have been getting together for nearly five decades to renew their friendship. This quilt was made for my mother-in-law, Velma Van Gerpen, who has always been a true girlfriend to me. Machine quilted by Becky Kraus.

The Garden *Kay Stotesbery, Bellevue, Washington, 1998. 44" x 42"*

This piece began as an attempt to display a favorite packet of old note cards that I have been hauling around for years. I like the bold, dark flowers—they are a nice change from pastels. I felt that a primitive-style block and quilting matched these blooms. I used pearl cotton thread to embroider the poem.

Happy Mother's Day *Sandy Bonsib, Issaquah, Washington, 1998. 15" x 26"*

This picture of my mother and me was taken when I was less than a year old. The quotation is one of my favorites and represents what my mother did for me and what I hope to do for my own two children. I chose light tan fabric as a background because it works well with the mood of the black-and-white photo. I used various shades of blue because it's my mother's favorite color. Machine quilted by Becky Kraus.

Mom's Bread *Sandy Bonsib, Issaquah, Washington, 1998. 65" x 61"*

For 18 years I have made a special homemade bread. It's our staple, a high-protein, whole wheat bread that my children have been raised on. My husband especially loves it, and worries that if something were to happen to me, he wouldn't know how to make it. So I photographed the bread in progress and placed the recipe on the back! Now he not only has the recipe, he also has pictures to help him. He has let me know that this is *his* quilt. Machine quilted by Becky Kraus.

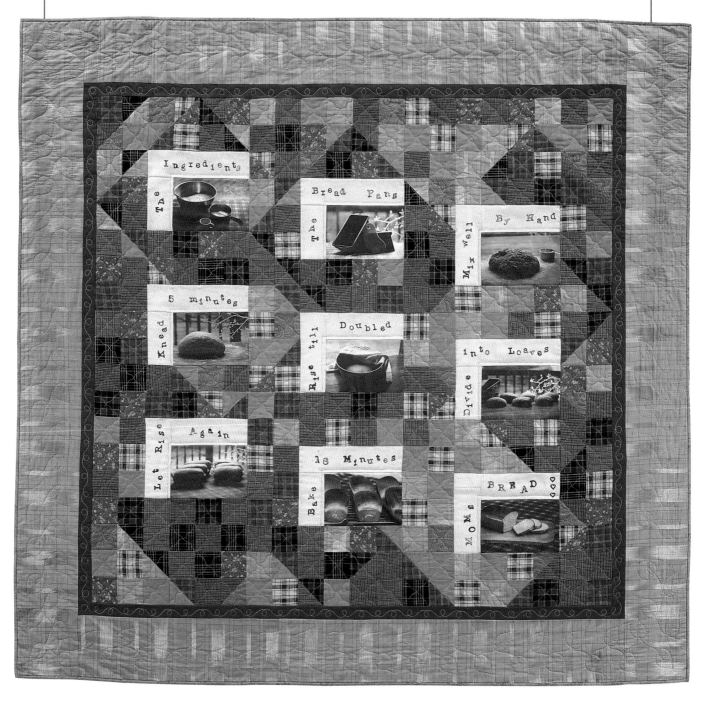

Hungarian Rhapsody *Ilona Doyle, Edmonds, Washington, 1998. 52" x 64"*

I made this quilt for my dad for Father's Day. I included photos from his first moments in America (from Hungary), just before jumping from a plane in Vietnam, his 25th wedding anniversary, and a few of the "big fish" that didn't get away! Machine quilted by Becky Kraus.

Mommy's Quilt *Kathy Staley, Seattle, Washington, 1998. 52" x 52"* ➤

I've always loved the symbol of the heart and hand; to me, it represents a mother's love for her children. The center was already completed when Sandy Bonsib suggested I add photos. I chose to put just a few on the front, and the rest were added to the back as if in a photo album. I love Kelly and Alex very much, and having their artwork and photos on the quilt is a great way to preserve my memories of their childhood. Machine quilted by Becky Kraus; hand quilted by Kathy Staley.

◄ *Feathered and Furry Friends* *Ursula Reikes, Ivins, Utah, 1998. 55^{1}/$_{2}$" x 59"*

One of the highlights of my life was being an animal keeper for one year and a weekly volunteer for six years at the Cougar Mountain Zoo in Issaquah, Washington. During that time I cleaned, fed, and photographed a wide variety of birds and mammals. This quilt features a few of my best friends at the zoo and is an important reminder that we humans share this earth with some magnificent creatures.

The Wild Side *Linda Petrick, Kirkland, Washington, 1998. 57" x 62"*

I made this quilt for J. Nelson, a contemporary painter, and it showcases some of his work. Jim uses bold colors and imagery that reflect Native American symbolism. These vivid colors bring contemporary life to a traditional quilt pattern.

Patchwork Farm *Sandy Bonsib, Issaquah, Washington, 1998. 55" x 56"*

We live on a small farm with our many animals, who bring us endless joy and laughter as we watch the babies grow and the pecking order develop. Skipper the Queen is our oldest cat. We just lost Lancelot, our chocolate Lab, last fall at the age of 14. Chuck, the baby chick, was hatched in a mother duck's nest, so he thinks he's a duck, hence the name Chuck. There's never a dull moment in the barnyard! Machine quilted by Becky Kraus.

◄ *Souvenirs of Turkey* *Elin Rodger, Seattle, Washington, 1997. 64" x 76"*

My three weeks in Turkey were full of rich experiences, and many are recorded in my photographs. Turkey is a tapestry of wonderful sights: ancient ruins, beautiful mosques, grand bazaars, colorful clothes, and blue Mediterranean waters. As a quilter, I was drawn to the craft of rugmaking. Beautiful rugs in all sizes were everywhere to be seen, touched, and purchased. The mini-rugs in the quilt are replicas of traditional patterns used in full-size carpets. It was great fun to combine three favorite hobbies—quilting, photography, and traveling—into one project. Machine quilted by Kathleen Steinke.

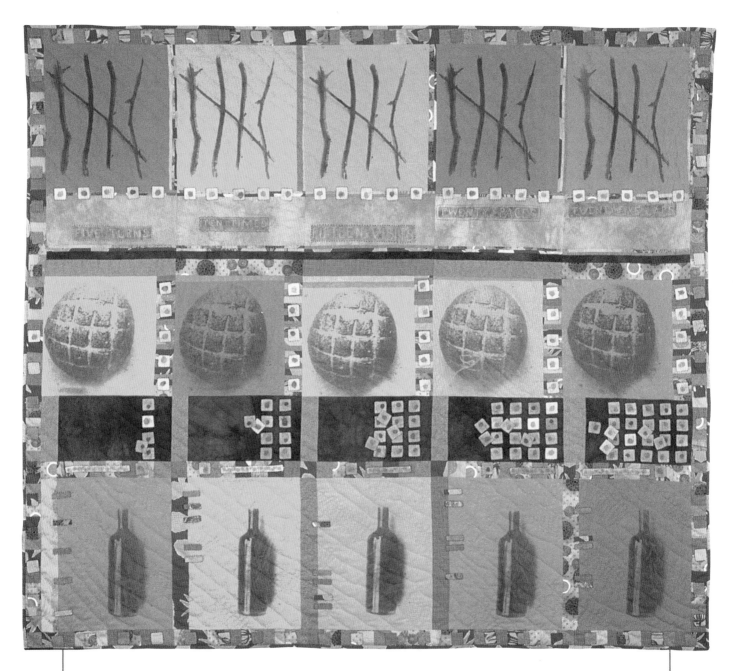

Keeping Track *Rachel Brumer, Seattle, Washington, 1994. 62" x 56"*

Life is a series of check marks, an accumulation of duties, routines, and pleasures. These are the essential elements of our days. We save empty bottles and photo albums. We measure our children's heights by scratching marks on door frames. We keep track.

Art Transformed and Original Works

This section features quilts with original artworks transferred to fabric, as well as quilt designs that are works of art in themselves. Art quilters use their own drawings and paintings or pieced designs to define a memory, reflect a mood, interpret a relationship, or make a social or political statement. Still others applaud nature and her beauty.

Repeat Block I: Neighborhood ➤

Gerry Chase, Seattle, Washington, 1993. 38" x 55"

I wanted to superimpose realistic architectural details onto my simple drawings of house shapes. While traveling in Scandinavia, I found exactly what I was looking for. I came home with rolls of pictures of stone, walls, wood siding, and roofs, plus shots of my husband draped with camera equipment (photo in the left border).

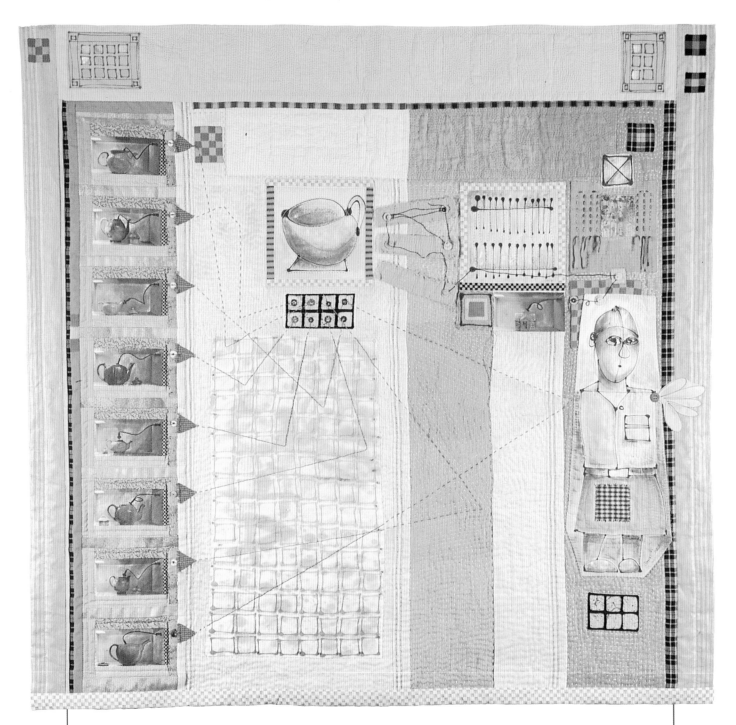

The Operator *Gerry Chase, Seattle, Washington, 1995. 47" x 48"*

While warming up a bit of tea, I got the idea to photograph some of my teapot collection inside the microwave oven. For two days the kitchen resembled a photographer's studio—cluttered with tripod, lamps, and other photography paraphernalia. Not much cooking goes on there anyway.

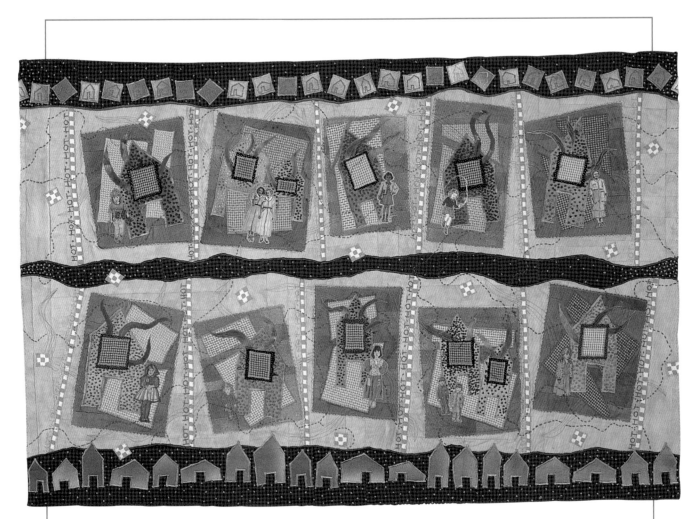

I'm Just an Ordinary Girl, and I'm Burning Down the House
Maude May, Seattle, Washington, 1997. 36" x 24"

Working late in my studio, I heard Bonnie Raitt sing her version of David Byrne's song, and this idea came into my head. The drawings are of women and girls who are important to me—some are real people, some are imaginary. All are powerful.

◄ *We Are Neighbors* *Wendy Huhn, Dexter, Oregon, 1996. 47" x 60"*

I worked with Clergy and Laity Concerns and local professional photographers to create a quilt depicting the women of Lane County, Oregon, and the stories of how they immigrated to the United States. This was a challenging piece to make—their stories were not simple. What I learned is that we are all immigrants, and we are all neighbors.

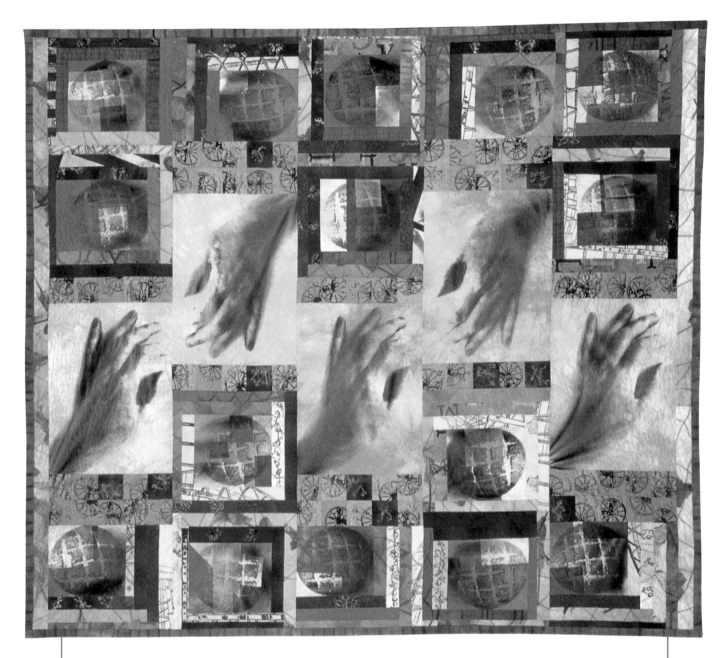

Long Associations *Rachel Brumer, Seattle, Washington, 1997. 78" x 69"*

The hand is a basic tool. Bread is a basic food. Shaking hands and breaking bread link us. In some cultures, breaking bread creates alliances and bonds of friendship.

A Banana for Breakfast *Barbara Barrick McKie, Lyme, Connecticut, 1997. 16" x 12"*

A sliced banana and cereal were placed on a computer scanner, and a bowl placed on top and then scanned. Later, the milk was added on the computer. The image was then transferred to polyester taffeta using sublimation transfer inks and a heat press. The knife used to cut the banana was also scanned and transferred. The banana was created out of hand-dyed fabrics.

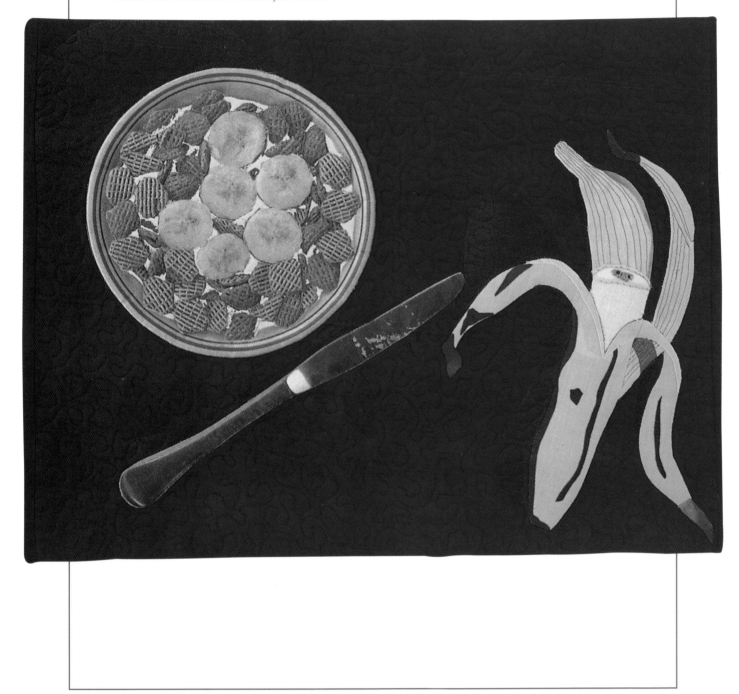

Chokeberry I *Deborah Melton Anderson, Columbus, Ohio, 1997. 11" x 15"* ➤

Several years ago I discovered an abandoned tile factory in Midvale, Ohio. The exterior walls were of galvanized metal, mostly painted red. One section, unpainted, had discolored from the blue-gray metal to mauve, gold, rust, and black. The crenulated metal and discolorations created the beautiful irregular stripes in the background of this image.

This piece contains three photographs only: two for the background and one for the brilliant red chokeberry leaves and bush. Tiny faceted black glass beads were added for subtle texture and color contrast. A single layer of transfer black is never black, but dark gray. Often a second pressing of dark images will produce black. Red, orange, and black machine embroidery threads were used to quilt the piece. All threads were pulled to the back and knotted, hundreds of them.

The Old Blacksmith Shop
Louise Slobodan, Nanaimo, British Columbia, Canada, 1997. 27^1/$_2$" x 18^1/$_2$"

This barn has housed a working blacksmith shop since 1949. It is still a working business and a most interesting site. After obtaining permission from the owners to photograph the building, I returned many times in October to capture the light at different times of day. I copied the photographs and played with them to arrange a composition. Next, the selected photographs were laser printed onto fabric, cut up, and reassembled in combination with hand-dyed fabrics. The border is a repeat pattern of old car springs leaning against the back of the barn.

Watch It

Wendy Lewington Coulter, Mission, British Columbia, Canada, 1992. 54$^{1}/_{2}$" x 60$^{1}/_{2}$"

This quilt is about the manipulation of minds by mass media, and by television in particular. I made it in response to the Gulf War, and most of the images within the TV screens are taken from media coverage of that event. The quilt examines the "manufacturing of consent" through television, and questions the dangerous practice of mistaking choice of programs for significant political choice. Placed in the context of an exhibition about women's work, this quilt looks at the connection between society's increasingly high tolerance for violence, and the experience of domestic abuse shared by so many women and children.

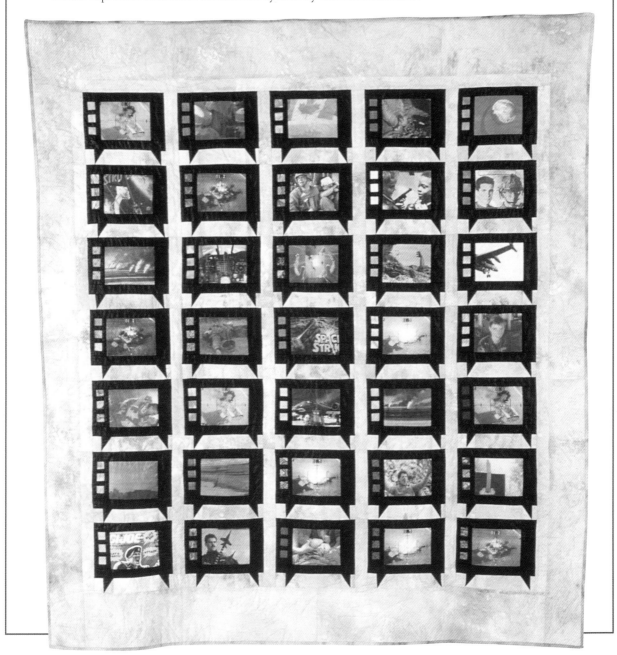

Forsythia O *Deborah Melton Anderson, Columbus, Ohio, 1997. 12" x 15"* ➤

Forsythia Series "O" was created using five photographs—two for the background and three of forsythia for the foreground. I enlarged the images (from 4" x 6" glossy prints) and transferred them to transfer paper, then taped the background together in sections. I cut the forsythia from transfer paper and attached them to the background with double-stick tape. The completed image was pressed onto the cotton cloth in two sections (because the heat press platen is only 14" square). I layered the quilt top with cotton flannel instead of the usual batting and backing fabric, then machine quilted with threads chosen to match or emphasize particular elements of the composition. Stretching the quilt onto wooden stretcher bars was the final step.

◄ *__Primavera__ Cathy Markham, Bellevue, Washington, 1998. 38" x 78"*

The photo transfers are the art of the 15th-century Italian Renaissance painter Botticelli. I have always loved his work. When the Italia line of fabrics was released, I was inspired to create this quilt. Machine quilted by Becky Kraus; hand quilted by Cathy Markham.

Our Teacher Is the Cat's Meow! *Pam Keller, Kirkland, Washington, 1997. 32" x 44"*

At Christmastime, students often give small gifts to their teachers. I thought it might be nice to combine the efforts of a class into one nice gift. As a quilter, it was easy to think of an idea! The students knew that Ms. Prather was fond of cats. I wanted the students to take part in making the quilt, so I decided they would provide the artwork. They each drew a different picture. It was fun to see how creative they all were. Needless to say, the teacher was delighted with the quilt. Machine quilted by Becky Kraus.

Children's Art

There is joy in preserving the art of our children—folk artists in themselves who often work with glee and abandon. And, of course, their art changes with time and age; the style of today will be gone tomorrow. Children make one-of-a-kind pieces we want to remember long after they have grown to adulthood.

Refrigerator Art Quilt *Jennifer Cockburn, Seattle, Washington, 1998. 28" x 38"* ➤

The idea for this quilt came to me when I was staring at my refrigerator, trying to decide what to cook for dinner. I realized that on my refrigerator were photos and drawings that I loved to look at, and I thought that making a quilt featuring some of my favorite photos would be a wonderful and indestructible way of preserving my refrigerator display. I used buttons and actual refrigerator magnets, leftover scraps of material, and small photos on this quilt. Machine quilted by Becky Kraus.

Framed Art *Diane Becka, North Bend, Washington, 1998. 14" x 12"*

These three pieces are individually titled Ashley's Bat, Samantha's Horse, and Colten's House. I thought that kid's art with a pieced border would make great place mats, but when my nieces and nephew didn't all make horizontal drawings, these wall hangings were the result.

◄ ***Budding Artists*** *Kathy Staley, Seattle, Washington, 1998. 41" x 56¹/₂"*

Whenever I go to my sons' school, I love to take time to admire the collages, murals, and artwork that cheer up the hallways and rooms. There is something so uplifting about children's artwork and the bright colors they use. Thanks to the photo transfer process, I was able to make a collage from the artwork my boys did in elementary school. Now I have a cheerful wall of my own! Machine quilted by Becky Kraus.

Ostling Family, Sweden *S. A. Williams, Seattle, Washington, 1998. 53" x 38"*

After seeing an appliquéd family history quilt in the Emigration Museum in Vaxjo, Sweden, I knew that one day I would make one for my family. Learning to put photographs on fabric inspired me to bring this concept to fruition. These are family pictures of my great-grandparents, grandparents, mother, and aunts in the area of Tallasen and Ljusdal, Sweden. The train ride between the two towns is seven miles. Family pictures of my relatives and the houses in which they lived, as well as the school my grandfather attended, are found here. I painted trees, flowers, and grasses on the quilt, then highlighted them with silk ribbon embroidery.

Telling a Story

These quilts use a storytelling approach. Some are tableaux with photographs, some are photographs juxtaposed with appliquéd symbols, and for those for whom a picture is not worth a thousand words, there are words to spell things out. The storytelling quilts are a creative way to pull together a particular theme—of hobbies, vacations, events, places, and dreams.

◄ *Santa & Me in '53* Mary Lou Weidman, Spokane, Washington, 1995. 41½" x 41½"

I remember having this picture taken with Santa. I was scared to death. My mother paid to have a recording of me talking to Santa, but I wasn't about to talk to that strange man. Mother was not very happy with her recording of dead silence. I can laugh about this story now, so I included the photo and other holiday symbols in a special Christmas quilt. Machine quilted by Pam Clarke.

North to Alaska *Linda J. Hunnell, Bellevue, Washington, 1998. 41" x 45"*

On vacation with my aunt, I took photographs of our experiences during a wonderful weeklong cruise to Alaska—a float plane landing on Walker Lake in Misty Fjords National Monument, a helicopter flying over Mendenhall Glacier, the ship at anchor in Sitka Sound, and icebergs calving off six-mile-wide Hubbard Glacier.

Our Childhood, *Kathy Staley, Seattle, Washington, 1998. 46" x 46"*

After doing Mommy's Quilt for myself (page 53), I wanted to make a quilt for my boys, Kelly and Alex, ages 12 and 10, to remind them of their favorite sports as children. They were an integral part of the planning, layout, colors, and title of the quilt.

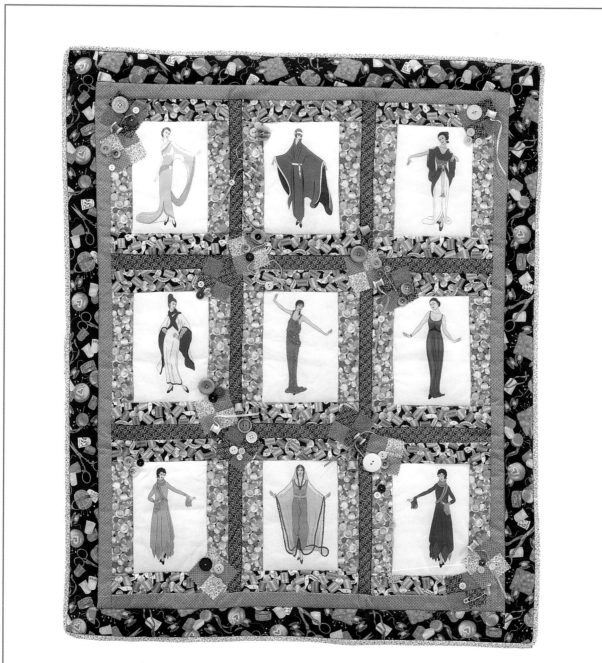

Fashion Design 101 *Joanne R. Fall, Seattle, Washington, 1997. 31" x 38"*

Instead of using photos I used clip art images of Art Deco fashion models. I framed the pictures to give them prominence. After the quilt was finished I embellished it with buttons, ribbon, and other sewing artifacts to accent the fashion motif.

Something Extra

This group of quilts is about adding something extra to the quilting process. Embellishment is a way to draw attention to and complement your subject, as well as adorn your quilt. Besides accessories and trims, embellishments can include fancy stitching and a variety of interesting threads. When it comes to adding these extras, creativity knows no bounds.

◄*Faces of the Garden* Holly Hollinger, Issaquah, Washington, 1998. 73" x 73"

This quilt was made for the annual auction for the Children's Garden School in Issaquah, Washington. Each class makes a quilt for the auction. The work of Ann Geddes, the Australian photographer, inspired this quilt. Each child's sweet spirit was caught on film, then transferred to fabric. Their faces then became all the wonderful things of the garden: a caterpillar, a butterfly, a ladybug, a spider, a dragonfly, and a bee buzzing through the beautiful flowers encased in pots. A birdhouse, pumpkin, mouse, gnome, and fairy give the finishing touches to the garden quilt. The teachers, Bonnie Steussy and Debby Smick, are represented as the sun and moon that give strength to the garden. The quilt is placed on the diagonal to give the illusion of looking into the garden from inside the school. Each mom used her imagination to create a one-of-a-kind square. Every type of embellishment was used. Batik fabric of green, turquoise, purple, and gold represent the colors of the garden, and a white-on-white print is used for the individual squares.

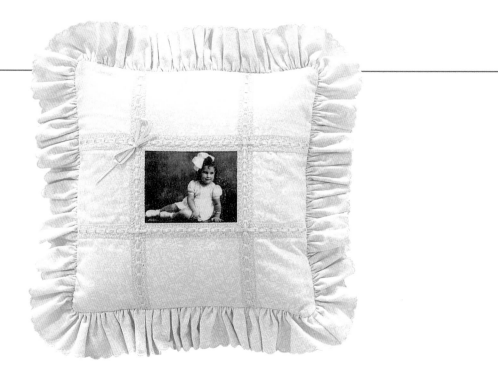

Mother's Day
Maria Groat, Bainbridge Island, Washington, 1995. 12" x 12"

My mother, Margarida Santiago, was always saying, "I don't have a good picture of you." So, one year for Mother's Day, I made this pillow using the last good picture of me—taken when I was three years old! This simple pillow in a Nine Patch format is made with white-on-white printed fabric, lace trim, and a woven peach ribbon.

Like Daddy *Maria Groat, Bainbridge Island, Washington, 1995. 13" x 20"* ➤

This quilt refers to a child's wish to be grown up—to aspirations, wishes, desires, longing for the adult world. The child wants to emulate her heroes, be in control of her destiny, and make a difference. I used a number of symbols in this piece. The music is very important to the people in the picture. The binding is finished on one side and not on the other to symbolize that the adult life is almost complete and he's learned a lot of lessons. The unfinished binding symbolizes the child—who has yet to experience life and has not learned its lessons. Different strings from the father's shop and ribbons from the child's collection are randomly tied together to symbolize the intertwining of their relationship. Ragged edges at the bottom of the quilt symbolize that the relationship hasn't always been smooth. Finally, the knot on the side symbolizes their commitment—that no matter what fate may bring, they will always be father, daughter, friends.

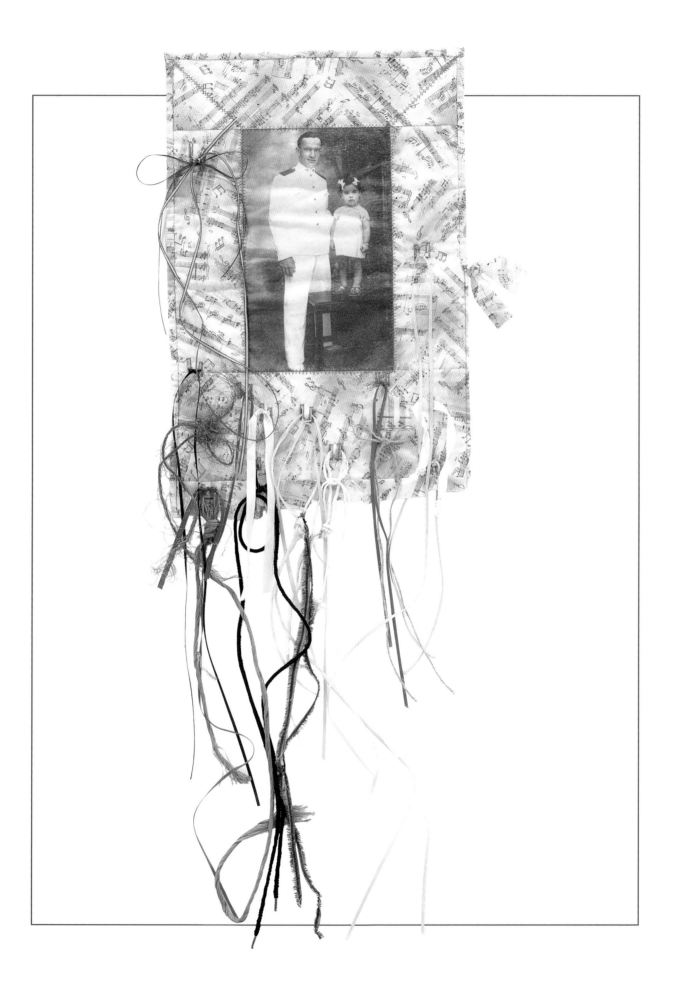

Kjeldsen Family Album *Irene Joshi, Seattle, Washington, 1998. 45" x 45"*

This quilt was made as a thank-you gift for my aunt, who generously loaned precious and rare family photographs for me to copy for use in the Kjeldsen family history project. It is set up as a genealogical chart, with her grandparents featured at the top, and includes the notices of their marriage and of her parents' births in the Danish parish where they were born. Her wedding photo is included, as are a number of snapshots of her siblings. She and her husband raised grand champion poodles, hence the poodle charm.

48 Feet *Wendy Huhn, Dexter, Oregon, 1996. 43" x 48"*

This quilt is an ode to my big ugly feet, which have always been a major pain. I embellished the quilt with beads, buttons, and mirrors.

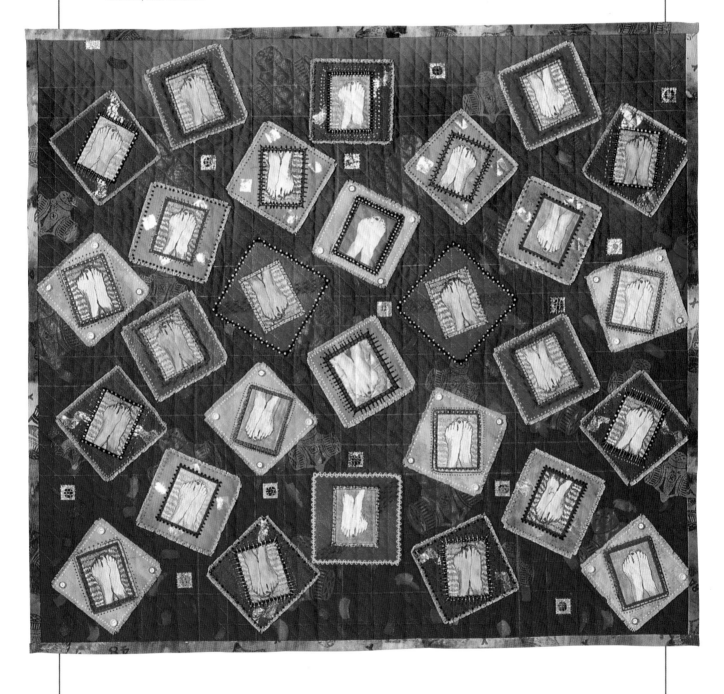

◄ *How to Survive Sixth Grade* *Irvina Russell, Duvall, Washington, 1998. 54" x 79"*

This quilt was made for my sixth-grade daughter, who loves to read. She wanted all her other favorite things represented, too. I was inspired by Wendy Etzel's book *The Collectibles Quilt*. I used the photo transfer process to make the plaques, photos and gold photo frame, Simplicity doll pattern, tape measure, badges and pins on the Girl Scout sash, and, of course, all the book titles.

Rich as Roses *Gail Patricia Hunt, North Vancouver, British Columbia, Canada, 1998. 53" x 53"*

This piece was made to celebrate my daughter Tess's friendships. Her best friend at age nine was Victoria. One day, the girls wanted to pose for photos to make a quilt, and one resulting photo of an overgrown rosebush at the beach was so beautiful that I decided to make a quilt myself. The rose is Tess's birthday flower, and we always have roses at her birthday celebrations. The hand quilting design, inspired by Carol Galloway's Viceroy butterfly quilting patterns, represents the life cycle of the butterfly, and symbolizes the growth and changes that a child goes through on the path to independence and maturity. Embellished with appliqué, confetti technique, hand embroidery, and three-dimensional flowers.

These Are a Few of My Favorite Things
Barbara Barrick McKie, Lyme, Connecticut, 1997. 18" x 18"

I used the computer to create "stamps" of the various things that members of my family and I collected for a challenge and group exhibit called Collective Fusion, sponsored by the Notrad online computer group (Notrad meaning "non-traditional"). The stamps were created from actual postage stamps, which have particular meaning because of what is on the stamp or the date or in most cases both, and from collectibles, such as thimbles, Christmas ornaments, and Civil War books. For the stamps, I made sublimation transfers onto polyester satin.

Ties that Bind *Julayne Capps, Tacoma, Washington, 1997. 73" x 48"*

My photo album quilt was created for my mother as a Christmas gift in 1997, but was designed to be an heirloom. It spans six generations on my mother's side of the family, with her as the focal point. I tried to give the quilt a Victorian look, yet include recent pictures as well as those from the past. I love to appliqué, so that became the technique of choice for my quilt. I put a lot of memorabilia on it, such as hankies that were my grandmother's, a glove of my mother's, and a Mother's Day card that I made in grade school. Lots of buttons and ribbons complete the look, and a large pink bow runs through the quilt to indicate the family "ties that bind" us together through many generations.

Scrapbooks and Albums

There is great simplicity in the scrapbook or album approach to quilting your memories. Many people just want to create a family record that they can display. Sometimes it's just too hard to limit the number of photographs you want to use. A scrapbook or album design provides a simple, attractive way to combine many images in one quilt.

When We Were Kids: Mystic Lake, 1952–1957

Karen Long, Seattle, Washington, 1998. 60" x 80" ➤

I made this quilt for my mother, Mabel Duffield. It represents memories of a very happy time in my childhood. We lived in a Montana Power camp over the mountains from Yellowstone National Park. To get to the lake, we had to hike three miles or ride the tram up the mountainside and then take a two-car train. The upper part of the quilt represents the lake itself; the lower part of the quilt is the power plant where my dad worked and we lived. The bears regularly raided our garbage cans, deer grazed outside our windows, and my sister and I would get up at 5:00 in the morning to feed the chipmunks. We went to a one-room country school. I was a seventh-grader when I arrived and the only one in my class. What a carefree time in my life! Machine quilted by Becky Kraus.

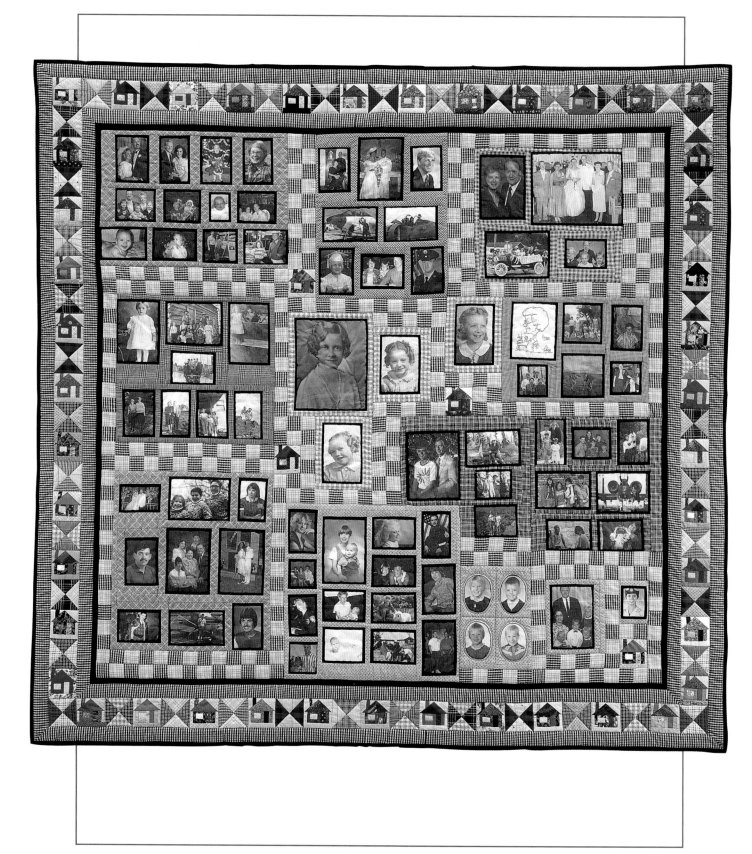

◄ *All My Children*

Judith Lindsay Griffin, Tacoma, Washington, 1996. 69" x 67"

About two years before Mom's 80th birthday in 1996, I began the process for this memory quilt. The goal was to include photos of all her children, grandchildren, and great-grandchildren and their activities. The center section has photo memories from olden days to present, while the top and bottom sections are grouped by family. The border consists of hand-pieced blocks made by several family members, including a great-grandson. On the back of the quilt, a schematic lists each picture by number, with dates, names, and locations. The label is a muslin square signed by all of the guests at Mom's birthday party. The quilt was a tremendous hit. It hangs in Mom's living room and remains the focus of family gatherings.

Memories *Kathleen S. Zeigler, Seattle, Washington, 1998. 50" x 63"*

I made this quilt for my mother, Marellen R. Stafford, for her 70th birthday. The time frame goes back to her great-grandparents, down through to her children.

75th Birthday Quilt *Sheila Guy-Snowden, Seattle, Washington, 1998. 42" x 60"*

This quilt was made to honor my mother-in-law's birthday. The quilt shows her in the top middle as a young woman, her marriage, her six children, her daughter's graduation, some of the grandchildren, and her favorite brother. The quilt was also made because one of her sons died. He was my favorite brother-in-law, and he had no children. Although she has many pictures of him, I thought it would be a special gift that she can pass to one of her children later.

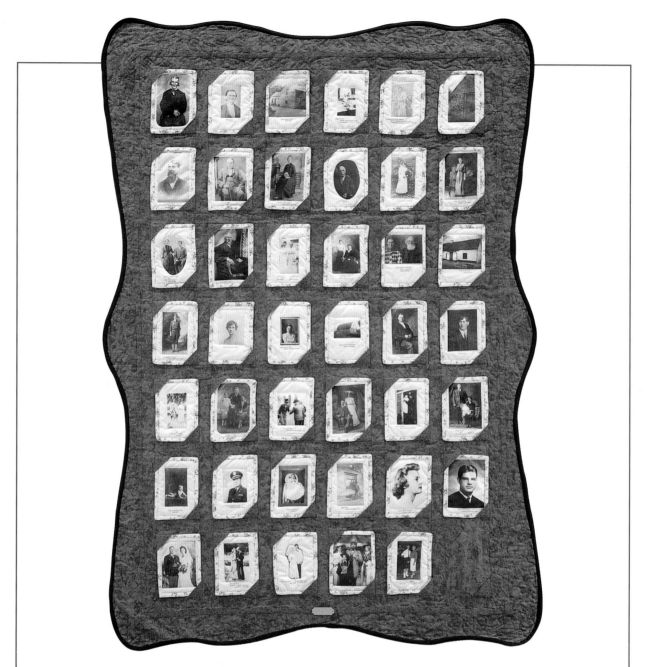

Scoby Family Album *Lynn Scoby, Shoreline, Washington, 1998. 50" x 70"*

My mother-in-law, Charline Scoby, wanted to do a genealogy tree of all of the old family photos for her authentic Victorian parlor. We stitched each photo into a mini-quilt, then inserted them into the "photo corners" on the quilt top. Pictures can be moved around, changed, or added. The last square was left blank to leave room for future generations. A great way to tell a story in pictures, this approach could be used for team pictures, a wedding, or an anniversary. Since there is a minimum of colors and pieces, this would be a quick project to do with a quilt buddy—one to cut and press, and one to sew. The curving edge was adapted from Cody Mazuran's book *A Fine Finish*.

Bibliography

Hopkins, Judy. *Around the Block with Judy Hopkins* Bothell, Wash.: That Patchwork Place, 1994.

Laury, Jean Ray. *Imagery on Fabric*. Lafayette, Calif.: C&T Publishing, Inc., 1997.

Milligan, Lynda, and Nancy Smith. *Photo Memories in Fabric (Book 1): Quilts and More*. Denver, Colo.: Possibilities, 1997.

Reikes, Ursula. *Quilts for Baby: Easy as ABC*. Bothell, Wash.: That Patchwork Place, 1993.

_____. *More Quilts for Baby: Easy as ABC*. Bothell, Wash.: That Patchwork Place, 1997.

Ritter, Vivian Howell. *Family Keepsake Quilts: Capturing Treasured Memories in Cloth*. Golden, Colo.: Leman Publications, Inc., 1991.

Simms, Ami. *Creating Scrapbook Quilts*. Flint, Mich.: Mallery Press, 1993.

Resources

Photo transfer paper:
Patchwork Northwest
18327 SE 60th Street
Issaquah, WA 98027
Phone: 425.644.7421
Fax: 425.644.1392

Cyanotype supplies:
Blueprint Printables
1400 Marsten Rd. #A
Burlingame, CA 94010-2422
Phone: 415.348.2600

About the Author

Sandy Bonsib made her first quilt in the early 1970s. Since then, she has become a well-respected quiltmaking teacher. She says, "For me, this is the best of both worlds, since teaching is my profession and quilting is my passion." This is Sandy's second book; her first book, *Folk Art Quilts: A Fresh Look,* was published in 1998. Sandy lectures and teaches for quilt guilds and conferences around the country. She lives in Issaquah, Washington, with her husband, their two teenage children, and many animals.

Books from Martingale & Company

Many of these books are available through your local quilt, fabric, craft-supply, or art-supply store. For more information, call, write, fax, or e-mail for our free full-color catalog.

Martingale & Company
PO Box 118
Bothell, WA 98041-0118 USA

1-800-426-3126
International: 1-425-483-3313
24-Hour Fax: 1-425-486-7596
Web site: www.patchwork.com
E-mail: info@patchwork.com

11/98